This journal belongs to

____

Published by
Puggy Pug life

9 781792 826658